LITTLE LIBRARY

Gymnastics

Christopher Maynard

Kingfisher

NEW YORK

Contents

Being a champion

Champion gymnasts today are also sports stars. National teams travel all around the world, often performing in front of huge crowds. This may seem glamorous, but the job is also hard work — gymnasts train day in, day out. A career at the top lasts about eight years, just until the gymnast's early to mid-twenties.

A career in gymnastics needs time and a lot of hard work. It takes a good five years to put together all the movements that are used in a champion's routines.

Long, long ago

Thousands of years ago, the people of Ancient Greece did gymnastics to train themselves for other sports, such as wrestling and jumping. But for many hundreds of years afterward, the only people to do similar exercises were acrobats. The modern sport of gymnastics is scarcely 200 years old.

A long time ago in China, acrobats performed tricks that needed all the strength and skills of a good gymnast.

In ancient times, gymnasts on the island of Crete did amazing acrobatic leaps over the horns and back of a charging bull.

In Europe during the Middle Ages, acrobats went from fair to fair doing balancing tricks and other gymnastic feats.

Competitions

An international gymnastics competition involves a great number of people and so takes a lot of organization. Teams from different countries around the world are invited, along with the coaches who train the gymnasts, and medical staff in case someone is hurt. There are also at least four judges for each event, plus a head judge.

THE TOP TWO

The Olympics and the World Championships are the two top competitions. Both last six days. The gymnasts perform twice — once doing exercises they've chosen themselves, and also doing ones set for them. The top 36 gymnasts then do extra exercises to decide the champion.

Equipment

The equipment at competitions tests all of the gymnasts' skills and strength. The contestants work their way around the floor, moving from one piece to the next.

The horizontal bar is the highest, up to 8 feet above the ground.

At the uneven parallel bars, one bar is higher than the other.

Both of the parallel bars are about $5\frac{3}{4}$ feet above the ground.

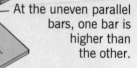

The women's vault horse is set sideways on.

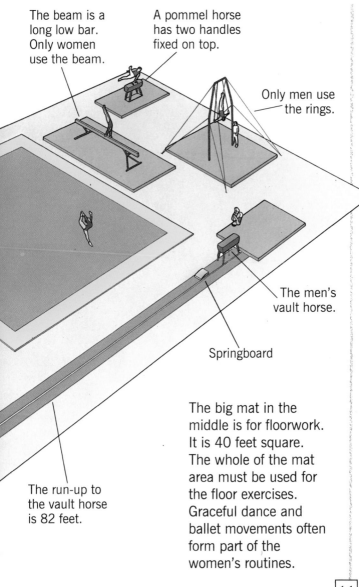

The beam is a long low bar. Only women use the beam.

A pommel horse has two handles fixed on top.

Only men use the rings.

The men's vault horse.

Springboard

The run-up to the vault horse is 82 feet.

The big mat in the middle is for floorwork. It is 40 feet square. The whole of the mat area must be used for the floor exercises. Graceful dance and ballet movements often form part of the women's routines.

11

Beams and bars

Gymnasts are allowed to stand, lie, or somersault over any part of the beam, as long as they don't touch the floor. They work along its whole length. It takes amazing balance to stay rock steady on the narrow top.

Working on the bars is difficult for beginners. Even the simplest moves take a lot of strength.

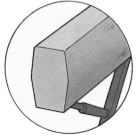

The top of the beam is only 4 inches wide.

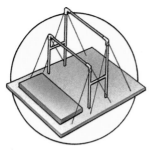

Uneven parallel bars

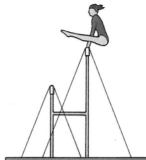

① On the uneven parallel bars, part of the routine is carried out on the high bar.

② The gymnast swings back and forth between the two bars.

③ The gymnast swings down to work on the low bar.

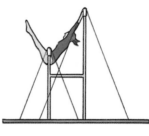

13

Vault and floor

Gymnasts run up to the vault horse really fast. Then they bounce off the springboard to give themselves extra speed. A handspring on top of the horse may be followed by twists or tumbles. Gymnasts finish by landing with their feet together and arms flung up and out wide for balance.

Springboard

FLOORWORK

Women gymnasts' floor exercises are carried out to music and include all kinds of leaps, tumbles, turns, and balances. In recent times, floorwork has become the most magical part of gymnastics, as graceful dance and ballet moves have been added to link the other exercises.

The vault is one of the first things beginners try when they start learning gymnastics. Speed and agility are needed to do well on this equipment.

In competitions, women are allowed two attempts at the vault, but only the higher score counts.

Bars and horse

U nless a gymnast has strong arms and shoulders, bar work is very difficult. These parts of the body have to carry and move the whole of the gymnast's weight.

Young gymnasts start out by working only on the parallel bars or the lower uneven parallel bar.

The horizontal bar is used for powerful and spectacular swings and circles.

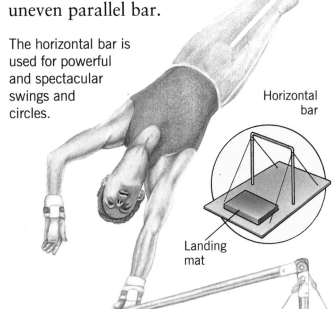

Horizontal bar

Landing mat

PARALLEL BARS

The men's parallel bars are of equal height. Gymnasts may pause to balance between swings. A balance must be held for at least two seconds.

As well as excellent timing and balance, gymnasts need great strength to perform on the pommel horse.

17

Rings, floor, and vault

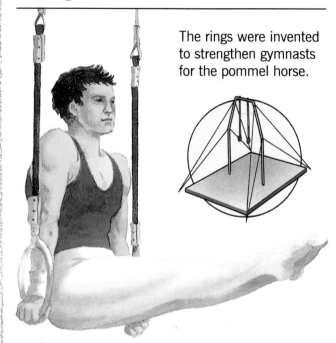

The rings were invented to strengthen gymnasts for the pommel horse.

Only men use the rings, and they must complete their routine without making the rings swing.

Men's floor exercises are shorter than women's and mostly show off strength and balance. There are few of the dance moves performed by women.

FLOOR EXERCISES

Men's floorwork isn't set to music. It is mainly made up of spectacular twists, somersaults, and balances.

The men's vault horse is set up lengthways, not sideways as for women. Men only get one attempt at making a good vault, not two.

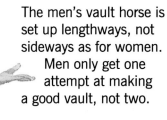

Rhythmic gymnastics

These graceful routines are set to music and performed only by women. The gymnasts use five different pieces of hand equipment as they move about the mat, showing a whole range of gymnastic and dancing skills.

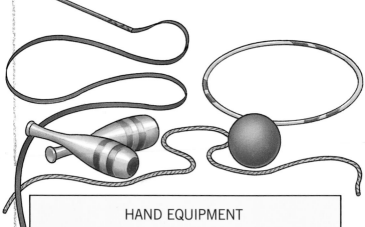

HAND EQUIPMENT

① The 20-foot-long satin ribbon looks spectacular as it flips and twists behind a gymnast.

② The hand clubs are made of plastic or polished wood.

③ Hoops can be any color except gold or silver.

④ The ball is plastic or rubber.

⑤ Ropes are often made of brightly colored nylon cord.

① The ball is always balanced on the palm. It must not be gripped with the fingers.

② Gymnasts may skip with the rope, jump through it, or simply throw it high and catch it.

③ The clubs are swung, twirled, and thrown up into the air, or bounced on the floor, or rolled.

④ Hoops may be rolled, bounced on the ground, or thrown high into the air.

21

Team gymnastics

R hythmic gymnastics can also be performed by teams of up to six women. In team events, the gymnasts can use more than one type of hand equipment. Each gymnast works with her own pieces, but she must also exchange them with other members of the team during the routine.

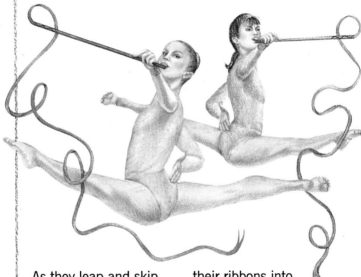

As they leap and skip across the mat, the women gymnasts twirl their ribbons into stunningly beautiful shapes and patterns.

TEAMWORK

Team events last for up to three minutes, much longer than solo routines.

The team must make at least six different formations on the floor during the performance. At times, the gymnasts display all of the grace and beauty of a troupe of ballet dancers.

The judges give marks for the way team members work together as a group, as well as for really original routines.

Acrobatics

Acrobatic gymnastics are like the shows you see when you go to the circus. Solo performers will do amazing tumble runs, with two or even three backward flips at a time. A team of gymnasts may make a high pyramid to show their strength and balancing skills.

The tempo routine is performed to music, with one gymnast being thrown by the others.

Teams are made up of two, three, or four gymnasts. They may be mixed, or men or women only.

The lightest gymnast usually balances on the very top.

Strong and supple

Gymnasts have to work hard to keep their bodies in shape. They have to practice special routines to make them as strong as weightlifters and as supple as ballet dancers.

Warming up muscles is very important, so start by slowly bending and stretching all parts of your body.

Sit with the soles of your feet together. Gently press your knees outward.

Back straight, toes pointed, stretch as far as you can along and between both legs.

Hands flat on the floor in front of your feet, straighten your legs as much as you can.

Knees bent, fold your arms across your chest. Sit up slowly keeping your feet flat.

Your feet apart, bend your front leg and lean onto it. Do the same with your other leg.

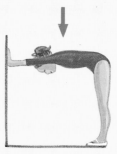

Hands flat on a wall, back straight, push your shoulders down as far as you can.

Hands flat again, lean your body into the wall. Then push off from it as if you were doing push-ups.

Squat down, then leap as high as you can with your feet together and your arms raised above your head.

Lie flat on your stomach on the floor, then gently lift your legs and arms to arch your back.

Your own routine

Inventing floor routines of your own can be great fun. You should only do this in a gym, however, with a properly qualified instructor to help you. Try out different dance steps, poses, and gestures in a mirror. Be sure to plan your moves so that you use as much floor space as possible.

MOVING AROUND THE FLOOR

① Start with a full-turn jump. Land with bent knees.

② Make this ballet shape, keeping your supporting leg straight.

③ Do a cartwheel.

④ Do a forward roll, using your hands to cushion the start.

⑤ Sit back, then roll into a shoulder stand. Use your hands to hold your hips high into the air.

⑥ Come down, roll over, and push up from a flat position.

⑦ Jump forward into a crouch, feet together behind your hands. Straighten up and finish with your arms held out high.

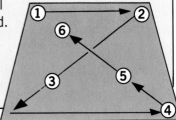

① Full-turn jump

② Ballet arabesque

③ Cartwheel

④ Forward roll

⑤ Shoulder stand

⑥ Push up, then jump into a crouch.

⑦ Finish

29

Index

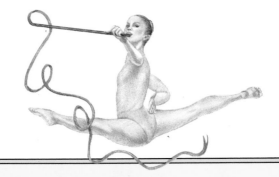